AF489298

To my son, Zaylen.

I understand how hard you try to fit inside the lines that society has drawn for you. I want you to know that I love all the unique things about you that make you who you are. You are incredibly special, and I can't wait to see where life takes you.

Love, Mommy

There is a boy named Z,
described as spirited and bright.

Soccer is his passion,
he plays with all his might.

But things don't always come easy for Z.
Because he has something called

ADHD.

A
D
O D
D D
E P D D
Y O E F E

At school, he bounces in his chair
and struggles to focus.

His energy is boundless,
he finds homework atrocious!

Home isn't much better,
always running down the hall.

He makes the biggest messes
and knocks pictures off the wall.

Controlling his energy takes all of his effort.
This makes Z angry
and his pounding heart hurt.

He feels like he's trying
but no one seems to notice.
There's always so much yelling,
he thinks, "This is so bogus!"

Meeting new people makes him
nervous and scared.

"Who is this person,
and why should I care?"

Crowded spaces
with so much noise and bright lights
are overwhelming to Z
and cause so many fights.

People think it's so easy,
so quick to call him "bad."
What they don't understand
is Z can't express why he's mad.

Something special, though,
happens when Z's on the field.
It's his safe space,
like a magical shield.

Everyone's in awe when Z gets the ball.
He sprints down the pitch,
so much faster than them all.

When his teammates need a sub,
he's always ready to go.
He can run and run and run,
until the ref's whistle does blow.

He juggles the ball
as the coach shares the play,
this helps his brain focus
on the strategy today.

Meeting new people is just part of the game.
New refs, coaches, teammates
every season he plays.
On the sidelines they cheer.
"Hooray!" they exclaim.

Z's love of soccer brings him so much joy.
He can shine as his true self,
such a happy boy.

What if he could use these same skills
at home and at school?

Embracing his energy
could be oh so cool.

He can ask for a break to get out his wiggles.
His frustrated friends
might even let out giggles.

And when it's time to listen
and sit still in his chair.
He can use a fidget toy
to clear his mind's foggy air.

He can turn boring tasks
into a fun racing game,
speeding through his chores,
leaving no time for blame.

8:88

When there's too much going on all at one time
there's no reason to panic.
Breathe in, think of soccer,
it can calm his mind.

Z's energy is a gift.
Something to be proud of, for certain.
He's in control of himself,
his ADHD's not a burden.

Z's journey taught him a lesson so grand,

being true to yourself

is where victories stand.